IMAGES
of America

CHICAGO'S
SOUTHEAST SIDE

Tom Shanley began employment for the Illinois Steel Company's South Works in South Chicago on September 7, 1893. He worked as a craneman in the Bessemer Department at the time this March 1936 photograph was taken.

IMAGES
of America

CHICAGO'S
SOUTHEAST SIDE

Rod Sellers and Dominic A. Pacyga

ARCADIA

Published by Arcadia Publishing,
an imprint of Tempus Publishing, Inc.
2 Cumberland Street
Charleston, SC 29401

Printed in Great Britain.

Library of Congress Catalog Card Number: 98-87775

For all general information contact Arcadia Publishing at:
Telephone 843-853-2070
Fax 843-853-0044
E-Mail arcadia@charleston.net

For customer service and orders:
Toll-Free 1-888-313-BOOK

Visit us on the internet at http://www.arcadiaimages.com

This postcard from the early 1900s shows seven religious institutions in South Chicago. They reflect the diverse religious and ethnic roots of the community, as well as the strong local identity of residents.

CONTENTS

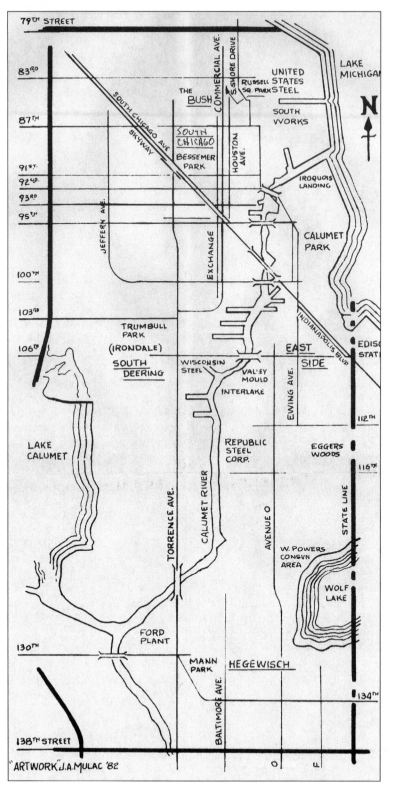

This map, drawn by resident Joseph Mulac, illustrates the four communities that make up Southeast Chicago. They are South Chicago, South Deering, the East Side, and Hegewisch. Also identified are major industrial sites and other landmarks in the area.

6

INTRODUCTION

Southeast Chicago is a geographically distinct place. Its boundaries, largely manmade, appear suddenly as the cityscape unfolds south from the Loop. Chicago's unbroken line of lakefront beaches and parks abruptly comes to an end where South Chicago's steel mills once stood, south of 79th Street. The housing shifts from the middle-class apartment buildings and massive single-family homes of South Shore to working-class two-flats and cottages. Southeast Chicago's four communities are South Chicago, South Deering, the East Side, and Hegewisch. Each community includes a series of neighborhoods, with names like The Bush, Millgate, Slag Valley, Irondale, Trumbull Park, Fair Elms, Jeffery Manor, Arizona, and Avalon Trails. The Industrial Revolution, and later, post-industrialization, have left their marks everywhere in this "city within a city." Each of Southeast Chicago's neighborhoods has been the home to various institutions, ethnic groups, and a variety of public spaces that defined them over time. All the neighborhoods have prospered, changed, declined, and been reborn under the smokestacks and church steeples that characterized this part of Chicago for over 150 years. Today, most of the large industrial plants are closed, as are many of the ethnic churches and schools. A way of life in Chicago has largely passed. The low-hanging dark cloud of smoke, which once signified prosperity, has all but disappeared from this and other American milltowns. Left behind are large industrial neighborhoods, full of history and waiting for another chance to play an important role in the city's and the nation's economy.

South Chicago was the first of these steel mill neighborhoods to emerge in the 19th century. Its early life is wrapped in legends, the most famous of which includes the story that an army engineer chose the mouth of the Chicago River as the location for Fort Dearborn, rather than the superior Calumet River location, because of his love for a fur trader's daughter. Whatever the reason, the fort was built on the banks of the Chicago River and the city emerged there, rather than to the south, on the Calumet. South Chicago owes its founding to the creation of the Calumet and Chicago Dock Company, which developed the area as an industrial site, despite its early existence as a home to the Potawatomi Indians and as a fishing village and fur-trading center. Originally called Ainsworth, South Chicago eventually became part of the Township of Hyde Park, as did all of Southeast Chicago. The town then joined the city of Chicago in 1889, along with the rest of Hyde Park. By that time, the steel industry had already begun to transform the district into a major American industrial center.

In 1875, the Joseph H. Brown Iron and Steel Company built the first mill in the area, on the east bank of the Calumet River, near 109th Street, in what became known as Irondale. Other manufacturers soon arrived. In 1880, the North Chicago Rolling Mill Company chose a site at the mouth of the Calumet River in South Chicago for its new South Works. The plant became part of Illinois Steel after an 1889 merger with two other firms. South Works grew to be the largest producer of structural steel in the world. In 1901 it became a major plant of U.S. Steel, the dominating corporation in the steel industry. In the 1890s, Iroquois Steel built a new plant on the East Side, and was soon joined by the Chicago Tack Company, further expanding the area's industrial strength. Both companies later evolved into larger steel concerns. Farther to the south and east, the United States Rolling Stock Company attempted to build a model industrial town, named after its president, Achilles Hegewisch, and patterned after Pullman, a neighboring town. The company later became known as the Pressed Steel Car Company.

The mills brought workers and their families to the banks of the Calumet. People of Irish, Swedish, German, English, Welsh, Scottish, and French-Canadian descent flocked to the mill neighborhoods. As these groups spread across Southeast Chicago, they created their own institutions, particularly churches. Catholic and Protestant parishes appeared all across the various mill neighborhoods. Parochial schools, saloons, social and athletic clubs, stores, libraries, and other commercial and meeting places abounded. As the mills expanded, so did the ethnic communities. Poles, Lithuanians, Slovaks, Slovenians, Italians, Croatians, Serbs, African Americans, and Mexicans all made their way to Southeast Chicago. Like other ethnic groups who had previously settled in the area, these groups added to the institutional base of the mill neighborhoods. This organizational foundation later provided support for labor unions, which made several unsuccessful attempts to band the workforce together. Finally, in the 1930s, organized labor came to be a permanent force in Southeast Chicago with the emergence of the United Steelworkers of America.

In 1980, Wisconsin Steel, in South Deering, closed its gates, and the wholesale abandonment of the district by steel manufacturers began. Years earlier, Youngstown Sheet and Tube had left its old Iroquois Steel plant, but the closing of Wisconsin Steel staggered the community. Wisconsin Steel included the old Brown Iron and Steel site, the first mill in the district. After 1980, the exodus of industry continued for 15 years. In 1992, the USX Corporation closed South Works. The burnt-red light of the massive blast furnaces no longer lit the night skies with an eerie, almost hellish, glow. The post-industrial era had dawned.

Since being annexed to the city, Southeast Chicago has played a central role in Chicago's economy and its social, ethnic, and political lives. The following images tell some of the story of this fascinating part of Chicago, detailing the economic and cultural institutions of a vibrant working-class community. While separated by ethnicity, religion, social class, and race, most residents of South Chicago were united by steel. These neighborhoods were milltowns in their own right, included within the boundaries of a great city. Steel helped to create Southeast Chicago, but as the new millennium approaches, its people will determine the future.

One
NEIGHBORHOODS

Southeast Chicago is a place of neighborhoods. They are shaped by ethnicity, social class, and by a physical presence that has always implied industrial might. The following photographs give views of South Chicago, South Deering, the East Side, and Hegewisch that should be familiar to current and former residents. Housing, commercial strips, historically important public spaces, and monuments recognizable to all help to mark the area as distinctive from the rest of Chicago. Bridges, alleys, parks, hospitals, theaters, train stations, the Chicago Skyway, and police and fire stations all identify the neighborhoods of Southeast Chicago. These public spaces helped to characterize the district both to residents and outsiders alike.

The working-class character of South Chicago and the other parts of Southeast Chicago is evident from the structures pictured here along the 9100 block of Exchange Avenue. The balloon frame two-flats and cottages erected on a 25-foot lot were favorite architectural models for developers of Chicago's industrial neighborhoods. Later buildings included brick and greystone building in this part of the neighborhood close to the commercial hub of Southeast Chicago.

The 92nd Street Bridge crossed the Calumet River and connected the neighborhoods of South Chicago and the East Side. This view of South Chicago from the East Side shows the oldest sections of the neighborhood, which developed along Harbor Avenue across the river. The scene also reflects the river traffic bottleneck, caused by swing bridges built on piers in the middle of the river channel.

Pictured here in 1912 is the South Chicago Police Station at 89th and Exchange Avenue. The city of Chicago built this structure in 1893 and operated it as a police station and branch court until 1981. It continues to serve the community as a comprehensive health center today.

Prior to the opening of the original South Chicago Hospital, sick and injured individuals had to travel 15 miles to the nearest hospital in Chicago. First, they rode on horse-drawn carriages to a steam engine train that took them to the city. The hospital was a welcomed addition to the community. It opened in the old Morgan Farm House, shown here, also known as the Adobe House, in 1900 with 15 beds.

A month after opening, South Chicago Hospital started a training school for nurses. According to its first student, Katherine Hamilton, "most of our cases were typhoid, pneumonia, or accidents from the shipyards." This is the class of 1937, which graduated 13 nurses.

Columbus Square is located at 92nd and Exchange Avenue. John B. Drake donated the memorial to the city in 1892. Originally located on the West Side, the city moved it to its present location in 1909. At various times, especially before the automobile era, the square provided a gathering place for residents and water troughs for thirsty horses. In March 1912, the square furnished a site for a reviewing stand during a parade that celebrated the visit of President William H. Taft to Immaculate Conception parish.

Three generations of the Majorgczyk family owned this house at 8355 South Baltimore Avenue in South Chicago. Pictured here in 1915, it stood in front of one of the railroads that serviced the South Works. Polish immigrants had a high rate of home ownership and pride in their property. Four members of this family owned this house over three generations.

Children's Play Ground.
Alley between Brandon and Burley Aves. looking north from 85th Street. Nov. 5th, 1918.

Chicago's alleys provided drives for residents to receive deliveries and have garbage taken away. Notice the lineman in the background. In industrial neighborhoods, many houses actually were built on the alley, sometimes sharing the lot with another house. As can be seen in this 1918 photograph, children quickly discovered that alleys supplied a place to play and escape from adult supervision.

The "Bush," pictured here in 1926, was named for the small scruffy plants found on the sandy soil of the area located near the shores of Lake Michigan. It was originally a favorite picnic area, but after the arrival of the South Works, it developed into a workers enclave, dominated until the 1960s by Polish immigrants. Some residents raised livestock here in order to supplement their incomes.

The 106th Street bridge crossed the Calumet River and connected South Deering to the west with the East Side neighborhood located across the river. A trolley car crossing the bridge and one of the many grain elevators along the Calumet River can be viewed in this 1912 photograph of a swing bridge.

Fire Station No. 51 stood at 10458 Hoxie Avenue in South Deering in 1912. Fire stations were important to the safety of neighborhoods, since most of the houses were constructed of wood. After the 1871 Chicago fire, the city limited construction of frame houses, but developers built them in outlying neighborhoods and outside the city limits. The Southeast Side was part of the Village of Hyde Park until 1889, when it was annexed to Chicago.

Each of the Southeast Side neighborhoods had a major park that provided recreational activities and facilities. The park field houses also supplied shower facilities for residents, especially before the widespread use of indoor plumbing. Trumbull Park is located in South Deering near Wisconsin Steel. In the 1950s, race riots rocked the park and surrounding neighborhood.

SOUTH PARK COMMISSIONERS

GENERAL PROGRAM of

Dedication

OF

Lyman Trumbull
Park 104th and Bensley Ave.

September 3rd, 1917

10:00 to 11:00 a. m. **Parade**

11:00 a. m. to 12:00 noon. Flag raising and patriotic speeches in different languages.

12:00 noon to 1:30 p. m. Lunch

1:00 to 5:00 p. m. **Band Concert**
Baseball Game
Athletics for Men and Women
Prizes offered to participants of community
Dancing
Tennis Matches (Finals)
Tug-of-War and other features.

8:00 p. m. Dedication services

These working-class cottages were located on the 10800 block of Hoxie in the 1920s. Most early residents of South Deering worked at Wisconsin Steel and lived in housing similar to these two wooden frame homes. Residents often used front and backyards to raise vegetables in order to help supply the family with fresh food.

15

Railroads played an important role in the development of the Southeast Side. Besides commuter trains, transcontinental trains stopped on the Southeast Side as they entered and left Chicago. This view from the early 1900s shows a young woman waiting for a train at the 100th Street Pennsylvania Railroad Station located in the East Side neighborhood at Ewing Avenue. The station and residential housing are visible in the background. Eventually, the railroad built a viaduct at this location in order to raise the tracks for both safety and traffic improvement.

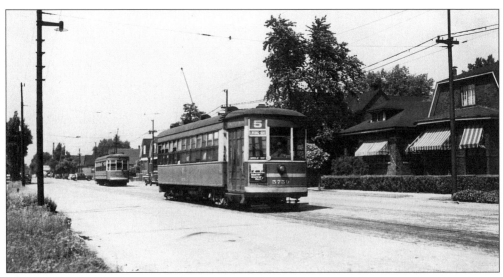

The "Number 5" street car shown here on 107th and Ewing Avenue connected the Southeast Side with central Chicago. Perhaps more importantly, it connected East Side residents with the Commercial Avenue shopping district in South Chicago. When local residents said they were going "uptown" they usually meant to Commercial Avenue.

Chicago built the "host house" for the 1933 World's Fair. This "welcome center" provided information to motorists entering Chicago on US Routes 41, 12, and 20, which passed through the neighborhood and linked the area to the eastern United States. It stood at 100th Street and Ewing Avenue on the site of the former Pennsylvania Railroad station. The Art Deco design of the building reflects the architecture of the 1933 World's Fair.

Douglas Taylor, an early real estate developer, lived in this East Side house with his wife who had inherited the property from an uncle. Taylor sold lots for homes in the area north of the Pennsylvania and New York Central railroad tracks and east of the Calumet River. The city tore down the building, which was located at 98th Street and the Lake Michigan shoreline, after a fierce lake storm damaged it. South Park commissioners built the Calumet Park Field House on the site in 1924.

The State Line Boundary Marker is probably the oldest surviving monument in the city of Chicago. Erected in 1833, it designated the boundary between the states of Illinois and Indiana at Lake Michigan. A similar marker placed on the banks of the Wabash River no longer exists. Commonwealth Edison, the East Side Chamber of Commerce, and the Southeast Historical Society restored the marker.

The grave site of Andreas von Zirngibl, an early German resident of the East Side, is located along the Calumet River at about 92nd Street. According to the headstone, he was a "one armed veteran of the Battle of Waterloo" who died in 1855. His last wish was to be buried on his land. A series of court battles protected his grave although the land around the grave has been owned by various industrial enterprises. The Southeast Historical Society and the Zirngibl family restored the grave, currently located in the middle of an operating scrap yard.

The following firefighters protected the East Side from fire in 1917: Captain Henry Dreyer, Lieutenant James Byrnes, Firefighter Conlies, Louis Kelly, Joe Einfeldt, Dan Lyons, Arthur Sullivan, John Pauregrau, Harry Swanson, Grant Lindstrom, Carl Aumick, and Fireman Schelain.

This is the funeral procession for East Side victims of the Iroquois Theater fire. The fire occurred on December 30, 1903, at a downtown Chicago theater. Almost 600 people lost their lives within 15 minutes in the fire, which claimed victims from most of Chicago's neighborhoods. Most of the dead were piled up in front of the exits, some of which were locked, while others had doors that opened inward and could not be opened against the crush of bodies against them.

The State of Illinois and the City of Chicago opened the Chicago Skyway in 1958 and connected the Indiana Tollway with the city. The Skyway collects the only road toll within the city limits of Chicago. The original toll of 25¢ has been increased over the years to $2. It parallels a transportation corridor, which includes a Native-American trail, a major railroad right of way, and a significant diagonal street, South Chicago Avenue.

This is a view of the East Side from the Albert Schwill Company looking west in about 1912. The dirt road in the foreground is Indianapolis Boulevard. Bethlehem Lutheran Church and St. Francis De Sales Church and School are pictured in the center of the view. Steel mills and grain elevators along the Calumet River are also identifiable.

The neighborhoods of the Southeast Side were suburbs of Chicago until 1889. Railroads that connected Chicago with the rest of the country made stops at local stations located in South Chicago, the East Side, and Hegewisch. The Hegewisch station of the Pennsylvania Railroad, shown here in a 1920 photo, was located at 133rd and Green Bay Avenue.

Illinois Governor Dwight Green unveiled a marker to dedicate Wolf Lake State Park on October 13, 1946. Wolf Lake is one of two state parks located within the city limits of Chicago. It is a recreational area where fishing, boating, and hunting are popular diversions.

This photo originally appeared in the *Hegewisch News*, a weekly community newspaper, on the occasion of the 1950 visit of Adolfo E. Hegewisch, nephew of the founder of the community. They are standing in front the Pressed Steel Company, originally known as United States Rolling Stock Company. Achilles Hegewisch originally founded the community in 1883. The entrepreneur hoped to develop a community loosely patterned on the town of Pullman, located to the north. Adolfo E. Hegewisch is shaking hands with Eugene Czachorski, editor of the paper, and Perry Hallberg, pictured to the left.

The Hegewisch Opera House opened in 1888 at 133rd and South Chicago Avenue, later Erie Avenue, and today, Baltimore Avenue. Many people traveled from surrounding communities in Illinois and Indiana to attend the various stage and musical productions held at the theater.

The State of Delaware built the Delaware House for the 1893 Columbian Exposition in Jackson Park in Chicago. After the fair, it was relocated by barge to the southwest shore of Wolf Lake in Hegewisch. The source of many colorful neighborhood legends, the house stood until it fell into a state of disrepair and was torn down in the 1950s.

This Hegewisch residence was also the location of the offices of Dr. Poehls, a family doctor. This photo typifies the housing that was common in Hegewisch, as well as recalls memories of the hometown family doctor who made frequent house calls and delivered babies in private homes. The closest hospital to Hegewisch was St. Margaret's, located in Hammond, Indiana.

A streetcar connected Hegewisch to the East Side and the rest of the city on tracks which ran over Hyde Lake. Commuters would take the one-track Hegewisch trolley with sidings for passing, and transfer to the "Number 5" at the East Side or South Chicago. This view shows the Hegewisch line being constructed through swamps of Hyde Lake in 1915. Hyde Lake no longer exists.

Settlers constructed the earliest residences in Hegewisch along Wolf Lake in the mid-1800s. This view shows the Neubeiser house at Wolf Lake in about 1930. The Neubeiser family was one of the earliest families to reside in the area that later became Hegewisch.

William Rowan served as alderman of the Southeast Side from 1927 to 1942. In January 1947, he won election to the United States Congress. Previously, Rowan had worked as a reporter and city editor for the *Daily Calumet*. A neighborhood park is named in his memory.

Max Stupar, a Slovenian-American from the Southeast Side, was an early aviation pioneer. In 1910, he organized the Stupar Aero Works located at 9626 Baltimore Avenue. In the same year, he built a 4-cylinder water-cooled hydroplane, which he hauled by wagon to 95th Street and Lake Michigan. A large crowd of South Chicagoans cheered him as the plane took off and he flew to Milwaukee. Stupar went on to have a long successful career in aviation.

25

The James P. Fitzgibbons Historical Museum (sponsored by the Southeast Historical Society) opened on Labor Day 1985. Present at the opening were Frieda Zimmerman, local newspaper columnist and benefactor, Jean Stanley, Frank Stanley, curator of the museum, Mildred Barnay, and Doe Stark and Lucille Waskiewicz in period costumes.

Many of the materials currently held by the James P. Fitzgibbons Historical Museum were collected by the Southeast Chicago Historical Project, sponsored by Columbia College/Chicago, the National Endowment for the Humanities, and the Illinois Humanities Council in the early 1980s. Pictured here is a film crew (Jim Klekowski, Michael Goi, Dominic Pacyga, and Michelle Crenshaw) under the direction of Project Director James R. Martin, conducting an oral history interview with neighborhood residents. Seated from right to left on the park bench are Alex Savastano, Dr. Romeo Palatto, Dan Delich, and "Buddy" O'Leary.

Two

COMMERCE

Commercial development followed quickly on the heels of industrial development in Southeast Chicago. The steelworker neighborhoods attracted various types of commercial ventures. Stores, restaurants, hotels, taverns, funeral parlors, and other enterprises quickly established themselves on the major streets of the district. While shopping and entertainment districts developed in all four of the community areas, the area near the corner of 92nd and Commercial Avenue quickly emerged as the Steel District's hub. The major banks, theaters, restaurants, and stores that served Southeast Chicago were all located here. Many of the commercial enterprises were ethnic in character. This proved particularly true of small neighborhood stores, funeral parlors, and the ever present tavern. All of these combined to give the steel mill neighborhoods a great number of meeting places where residents could meet to discuss life in Southeast Chicago and their work in the mills.

The crowded intersection of 92nd and Commercial Avenue is pictured here in 1912. These streets were busier than most small and medium sized American downtown streets. Well served by public transportation (even continental railroad passenger lines stopped nearby), 92nd and Commercial Avenue proved to be the heart of the Steel District. Residents could buy both necessities and luxury goods or enjoy a night out at a theater, restaurant, or social gathering.

Each of the neighborhoods had their own strip shopping district. Torrence and 108th Street was the location of the South Deering shopping district. Directly across the street from the Wisconsin Steel Mill, most of the businesses were family owned specialty shops. They provided goods and services to neighborhood employees and residents.

At the turn of the century, the original East Side shopping district was located near 100th Street and Ewing Avenue near the railroad station. This view looks north on Ewing Avenue from 100th Street. Numerous small businesses are visible, as well as the trolley car tracks running down the middle of the street and the railroad tracks in the foreground. In later years, the main East Side shopping area moved south to 106th and Ewing Avenue.

The heart of the Hegewisch shopping district at Baltimore Avenue and 133rd Street is pictured here in about 1900. This view shows the Opera House to the left and other small businesses located along the dirt street. The shopping district was particularly important to Hegewisch residents because of the geographic isolation of the neighborhood.

The Lederer Department Store, pictured here in 1920, dominated the intersection of 91st and Commercial Avenue in the South Chicago shopping district from 1895 until Goldblatt Brothers purchased it in 1927. After a fire during the Great Depression, Goldblatt Brothers built a new store at the location.

The C.R. Cave Department Store, located on East 92nd Street near Houston Avenue and pictured here in 1920, sold clothing and groceries as well as pianos, stoves, rugs, furniture, and many other household items. This firm also offered "on time" purchases.

The Goldblatt's Department Store, situated on the southwest corner of 91st and Commercial Avenue, was probably the most important establishment in South Chicago's shopping district and one of the company's most profitable stores. This 1950 view of the Art Deco structure shows the street and sidewalk traffic around the store.

Neighborhood banks provided financial services for area residents and local businesses. One of the most important financial institutions in the district, South Chicago Savings Bank, still stands on the southwest corner of 92nd and Commercial Avenue. It is visible in the top left hand corner of this 1934 photograph..

Members of the South Chicago Kiwanis Club gathered in front of the Steel City Bank of South Chicago, located at 92nd and Houston Avenue, after a Christmas party in 1945. At one time, a radio station (WJOB) broadcasted from a studio located in the bank building.

The Union State Bank operated at 92nd and Baltimore Avenue. Driven by the mills, the local economy supported several banks and savings and loan associations. This bank, pictured in 1917, closed during the Great Depression in 1933. The building fell into disrepair in the 1980s. A local community group, the United Neighborhood Organization (UNO), restored the building with its cast-iron facade.

The East Side Trust and Savings Bank stood in this impressive building located at 101st and Ewing Avenue. The bank opened in 1919 and also closed during the Great Depression. The building, with its neo-classical accents, now houses an auto parts store.

The Vaudette Theater operated as a small storefront theater at a location on 92nd and Houston Avenue. In the 1920s, the Vaudette showed silent films with Polish title cards.

Vaudette Theatre

92nd and Houston
H. L. HEISLER, Proprietor

Latest Pictures   **Good Music**

5c   5c

MR. CHAS. HOWARD, Character Entertainer
In up-to-date popular songs
DON'T FAIL TO HEAR HIM

At one time, 17 theaters operated across the Southeast Side, although none are still in operation. They have been replaced by theater complexes in suburban shopping malls. The Commercial Theater, located on Commercial Avenue on the 9100 block, was one of the largest and most popular neighborhood theaters.

The Gayety Theater and Ice Cream and Candy Store was a neighborhood landmark located at 9211 South Commercial Avenue. As the Mexican community in the area grew, the Gayety changed its format to offer Spanish language films. James Papageorge, a Greek immigrant who came to the United States in 1904, founded Gayety's Candies and Ice Cream. The theater burned down in 1982 and the ice cream and candy store continued its business in the suburb of Lansing, Illinois.

The East Side Theater operated at 105th and Ewing Avenue. This 1950 view advertises the air conditioned comfort of the theater. In the days before it became commonplace, many early movie theaters were the only places where area residents could enjoy air conditioning. Entrepreneurs built the theater in the mid-1920s. It was one of the first in the city to be converted to "talkies" later that decade.

The South Chicago Hotel and Restaurant stood near 92nd and Commercial Avenue in 1916.

In 1916, the Paris Restaurant fed hungry steelworkers and residents from their location at 9216 South Commercial Avenue. The restaurant stayed open through the night at a time when the steel mills operated around the clock with two 12-hour shifts. The steel industry had a direct effect on community businesses and local economic conditions; whenever the mills closed or cut back on their workforce, local concerns suffered and often closed.

The White Kitchen Restaurant is pictured here in April 1941 shortly before the American entry into World War II. The prices reflect Depression-era economics. Wartime inflation and prosperity soon brought price increases. This restaurant operated at the foot of 89th Street near the South Works general offices.

Milan's Restaurant and Pizzeria in Hegewisch served customers in the former Opera House building located at 133rd and Baltimore Avenue. The family remained in the restaurant business in Southeast Chicago for over 50 years. They later built a larger, more elegant restaurant and lounge at 9550 Colfax Avenue.

Walton's Headquarters stood on 92nd Street in South Chicago. Pictured here are Mr. Shepard, the bartender, and a customer standing near the entrance. Many taverns or saloons offered meals to the huge workforce in the area. Friday night fish fries were also popular, especially with Catholic customers.

Kurnik's Tavern served the Hegewisch neighborhood from a location at 13200 Houston Street. Many different types of taverns operated in the area. Some catered to particular ethnic groups. Some were largely "men only" establishments, while others were "stand up establishments" as shown here. Kurnik's stood across the street from another neighborhood institution, St. Florian's Polish Roman Catholic Church.

Pictured here is the Slag Valley Saloon in South Deering. Neighborhood saloons and taverns were more than drinking establishments. They provided centers of neighborhood social life, places where people met away from work and family. Many also provided rallying places for neighborhood political organizations.

Kinney's Marble Rail Bar served customers at 92nd and South Chicago Avenue. Neighborhood taverns often catered to families.

In 1918, the Dolatowski family opened this cigar and candy store at 8409 Burley Avenue in the "Bush" area of South Chicago. This interior view of the store shows Frank Dolatowski and his godfather, Frank Mularski. Ethnic entrepreneurs opened numerous small businesses to serve the immigrant community.

The Aniol and Hasiak Butcher Shop is pictured here in a turn of the century view. The Aniol family has been involved in several Hegewisch businesses, and currently operates a hardware store in the neighborhood. Note the soot marks on the ceiling from gas lights.

The Herndobler General Store, pictured here in 1892 at 10312 Avenue N, was typical of the many "Mom and Pop" grocery stores located on the Southeast Side prior to the development of large chain stores. Owners often let customers put purchases "on the book" until payday.

The George Willy Hardware stood at 10550 South Ewing Avenue in about 1915. Hardware stores often provided gathering places for local men to gather to talk sports, gossip, and play cards.

Murphy's Grocery Store operated at 13559 Burley in the Hegewisch neighborhood. Later, the store became part of the IGA (Independent Grocers of America) chain and moved to larger quarters on the 132nd block of Baltimore Avenue.

This 1905 view shows the proud owners of Brody's Clothing Store outside their establishment at 13309 Baltimore Avenue.

S. Pacini and a local newspaper vendor are pictured here at a newsstand at 92nd and Baltimore Avenue in 1920. The Pacini family owned a series of small stores in South Chicago and later in the East Side. This photo was taken right outside the second Pacini store.

Justin Cordero was one of the first Mexican immigrants to the Southeast Side. At first, Cordero worked in the steel mills. He later opened his own business, Cordero's Radio Shop, located at 3315 East 89th Street in South Chicago, shown here in a 1938 photo.

The Osterberg Coal Yard functioned at 100th Street and Avenue L in 1911. This photo shows a wagon used to sprinkle water on the East Side's dirt streets to minimize dust. The Osterbergs were early members of the East Side Swedish community.

The Daniel Jordan Supply Yards stood on Brandon Avenue in Hegewisch. At the turn of the century, people in their horses and buggies went there for supplies. The yards sold building supplies and bulk materials.

This photo of S.A. Livingstone Horse Shoer *c.* 1900 reflects a business no longer seen in city neighborhoods but which was crucial prior to automobiles becoming commonplace. Notice the high entrance which allowed carriages to enter the shop for repair.

The milkman was a familiar figure in neighborhoods, often treated like a member of the family. The F. Wilcken Dairy catered to the Southeast Side in 1902.

This is a 1930 view of a Shell Oil gas station located at 10550 South Indianapolis Boulevard near the state line between Illinois and Indiana. Indianapolis Boulevard (U.S. Routes 41, 12, and 20) provided a main route into Chicago from the east.

Owned and operated by the Neubeiser family, one of the neighborhood's earliest families, Neubeiser General Auto Repair served customers at 131st and Avenue O in Hegewisch. Avenue O connected Hegewisch with the East Side and the south suburbs of Chicago.

Farmers markets and neighborhood produce peddlers sold produce to local residents. This photo shows Market Day at 106th Street and the Calumet River in 1915. The factory and railroad tracks in the area did not discourage local shoppers.

South Chicago merchants held this sidewalk sale in 1982. This event occurred annually, bringing merchants and shoppers together in an open-air market on the sidewalks of the Commercial Avenue shopping district. This view of the 9000 block of Commercial Avenue reflects the ethnic changes which had taken place in the community by that time.

Three

INDUSTRY/LABOR

Industry, particularly steel, provided the heart of Southeast Chicago's economy. From the opening of the Brown Steel Mill in 1875 to the closing of U.S. Steel's South Works in 1992, steel remained the defining symbol of these communities. The steel mills cut most of Southeast Chicago off from the lakefront, but their presence was always evident. The glow of blast furnaces lit the night sky and the pollution from the mills covered the area with a rust colored dust. The sounds of steel making shook residential areas like the Bush or Irondale located next to the massive mills. By World War I, Southeast Chicago and nearby Gary combined as a major steel center. However, the steel industry was not the only employer in the area. Other industries also employed residents and occupied important places in the local economy.

Southeast Chicago developed as a major focus of the labor movement. Eventually, the union movement gave birth to the Amalgamated Association of Iron and Steel Workers in 1876. This organization's power peaked in 1891 with 24,000 members. Soon afterwards, the Amalgamated fell on hard times. World War I brought a successful union drive to the Chicago District. In 1919, however, steelworkers lost another bloody strike. After this conflict, unions disappeared in the Chicago mills until the 1930s when the CIO's organizing drives resulted in the successful creation of the United Steelworkers of America (USWA).

Pictured here are Pressed Steel workers in Hegewisch during a World War I Liberty Bond rally in 1918. Southeast Chicago workers played crucial parts in the various wars that the United States has fought over the last 100 years, both as soldiers and as war workers.

In 1880, North Chicago Rolling Mills established a steel mill at the mouth of the Calumet River where it flows into Lake Michigan. At various times, it was named Illinois Steel, Carnegie Steel, and finally United States Steel South Works. The South Works developed into the largest mill in the area and at its peak, employed just under 20,000 workers. This postcard view of the mill shows black smoke coming from the smoke stacks of the mill, then considered a sign of prosperity, not of pollution.

This 1885 view shows Blast Furnaces #1–4 at South Works, the first furnaces built at the mill. They stood near the south slip close to the Calumet River where lake boats brought iron ore, coal, and other natural resources to the mill.

This interior view of the employment offices at Illinois Steel Company depicts job applicants and mill employees including plant security. The multiple languages on the sign reflect the variety of non-English speaking immigrants who applied to work in the mills. The theme of the message is that the mill wants to hire workers who are safety conscious.

The schedules of the mills affected the entire area. The noon hour, other meal times, and shift changes had an impact on local traffic, businesses, and residents. Pictured here are workers from the South Works breaking for lunch in about 1910.

Albert Crouse, master mechanic, and the Rail Mill Crew posed for this photograph in 1890. South Works provided a model of modern technology and leadership in the production of high quality steel. The Rail Mill produced track for the nation's burgeoning railroads in the late 19th century. Structural steel from South Works provided the frames for many of the nation's skyscrapers.

This photo shows the Electric Repair Shop at U.S. Steel South Works in about 1960. This shop was particularly important in later years as the technology of steel making changed from the Bessemer process, to open hearth furnaces, electric furnaces, and finally basic oxygen process furnaces.

This overhead ladle crane was located in the #2 Open Hearth furnace, at the north end of the mill. The crane carried molten steel from the furnaces to the ingot molds below. It opened in 1904 and closed on Christmas Day 1965. It took about seven hours to make steel in an open hearth furnace.

This is a 100-ton crane constructed by the Machine Shop at South Works. The machine shop made tools and parts to repair equipment used in the mill.

Industrial accidents occurred frequently and often proved fatal. In 1906, 46 men died in accidents at Illinois Steel's South Works plant. Doctors at the plant hospital reported that there were at least 2,000 accidents a year during this period. South Works began to emphasize safety as reflected in this symbol. Organized labor often demanded more safety procedures in the mills.

In 1905, Robert J. Young began a study of injuries at South Works. The following year, the South Works Safety Committee recommended 3,000 changes in plant operations. U.S. Steel began a safety program in 1908 based on the South Works model but for the entire corporation. In 1890, the early and primitive net safety mask provided some protection for a worker.

The South Works organized the Goodfellows Club in 1912 for employees, providing social and charitable activities for members. Illinois Steel supported it as part of its welfare program to improve both work conditions and public image. One of the community's favorite events was the circus brought to South Chicago by the Goodfellows Club.

U.S. Steel organized many activities for its workers such as sports teams, singing groups, and even a Blast Furnace Band, shown here in 1918.

This view shows the South Works in 1947. At night the steel pouring process lit up Southeast Chicago's sky. The mills operated around the clock, seven days a week, holidays included.

This photo of a South Works parking lot taken in the late 1940s reflects the development of the automobile as a primary means of transportation for mill employees. In earlier periods workers walked to work from surrounding neighborhoods or used public transportation. The automobile made it possible for mill workers to live outside the neighborhood, even in the suburbs, and to commute to work.

54

The North Chicago Rolling Mill Company chose the site for South Works because of its proximity to water transportation. Gigantic ore carriers transported iron ore, limestone, and coal to South Works. They unloaded their cargoes at slips served by huge overhead cranes. The ship pictured here is unloading its cargo at the North Slip, which connected the mill to Lake Michigan.

This aerial view of the "Bush" neighborhood near U.S. Steel's South Works in about 1970 shows many of the important elements which built the neighborhood. In the center foreground sits Russell Square Park. Across the street is Sullivan Elementary School, and in the center stands St. Michael Polish Catholic Church. At the top of the scene is the mammoth U.S. Steel South Works plant with Lake Michigan in the background. The residential housing of the neighborhood is visible throughout the view.

Although this appears to be a police department roll call, in reality it as a photo of U.S. Steel plant security personnel. Like a city within a city, South Works had its own security force, fire department, ambulance, and medical clinic. It also had its own power plant for electrical power.

Illinois Steel Company hosted an anniversary dinner for workers with 25 or more years employed at South Works. This is a photo of the 1929 dinner held on November 24. U.S. Steel closed the plant in 1992 after 112 years of operation. Almost 600 acres of land remain vacant and for sale at the present time.

The Joseph H. Brown Steel Company, precursor to Wisconsin Steel, opened the first Southeast Chicago mill in 1875. After Mrs. Brown sold the property, a siren blew at 4:30 p.m. daily in memory of Joseph Brown. This aerial view shows Wisconsin Steel in 1948. Torrence Avenue separated the mill from the surrounding neighborhood, which was originally called Irondale, and its businesses and houses.

The molten refuse from the steel making process is called slag. Rail cars dumped the slag from the mill in a field where it cooled before being used for various byproducts. The neighborhood near Wisconsin Steel's slag dumping area came to be called "Slag Valley." This is a 1960 photo of slag dumping.

Pictured here are blacksmith Luigi Santangelo and his helper at Wisconsin Steel. Much of the labor in the steel mills was heavy manual labor. If a person had a strong back and the will to work hard they could earn a decent living in the mills. Higher education was not needed to obtain a well-paying job on the Southeast Side.

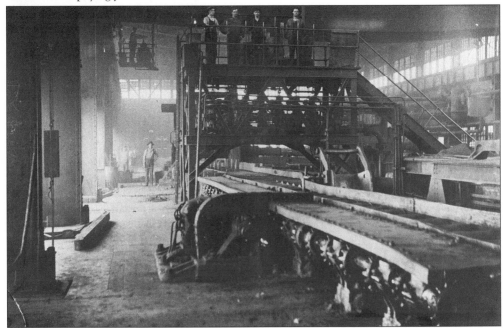

This Wisconsin Steel rolling mill, pictured here in about 1918, reduced the size of steel bars that were then sent to the straightening machine.

The photograph of the locked gates of Wisconsin Steel in 1982 reflects the harsh realities of plant shutdowns and worker layoffs that accompanied the decline of the American steel industry in the 1980s. Wisconsin Steel's precursor, Brown Steel, was the first steel mill to open in the area in 1875, and also the first major plant to shut its doors.

Wisconsin Steel closed in 1980 leaving 3,500 workers unemployed. The site is still undergoing cleanup and remains unused today.

In 1883, E.W. and O.N. Hutchinson founded the Grand Crossing Tack Company to make carpet tacks. Their small plant, shown here, operated at 79th and South Chicago Avenue. As the business prospered and expanded the Hutchinsons, decided to produce their own steel and built a mill on east bank of the Calumet River in 1902.

In 1916, Interstate Iron and Steel of East Chicago bought the Grand Crossing Tack Company. In 1930, Interstate played a role in the merger that created Republic Steel. In 1984, Republic Steel merged with J & L Steel to form LTV Steel, a subsidiary of the LTV Corporation. This view looking north toward the mills of South Chicago shows the Calumet River on the left and Avenue O and the East Side neighborhood on the right.

Industrial development in Hegewisch began with the United States Rolling Stock Company, which built railroad cars. The factory was located south of Brainard Avenue at the southern limits of the city of Chicago. After its failure, Western Steel Car and later the Pressed Steel Company replaced the company. Both of these firms also produced railroad cars. This is a view of the yards of Western Steel in about 1918.

A group of workers stand in the yards at Western Steel Car in about 1918. Achilles Hegewisch, president of United States Rolling Stock Company, loosely patterned the neighborhood on the nearby town of Pullman. His company, however, never had the control over the community that the Pullman Company exerted over its company town.

These men worked in a railroad yard behind 83rd and Baltimore Avenue. The railroads linked the many industries that thrived in the area.

The crew of Engine 27 pose in front of their locomotive. In recent years, many of the railroad right of ways in the community have been abandoned. Some are being creatively adapted to use as hiking and biking trails.

The Albert Schwill Company operated on the East Side. Later, the Falstaff Brewing Company purchased the site. This view looking toward the southwest shows the Calumet River in the background. Also in the background are steel mills and grain elevators.

The launching of the steamship *Manta* occurred in 1915. Shipbuilding in shipyards along the Calumet River provided another important local industry. Area shipyards repaired lake boats. A rooming house district developed near the shipyard for sailors.

The General Mills Plant in South Deering operated at 104th Street and the Calumet River. Water transportation proved crucial to the decision to build at this location. The plant produced Wheaties, Cheerios, and other breakfast cereals. The Rialto Grain Elevator, a flour mill, and a cereal plant were all located on the site pictured here. Recently, this factory closed.

The port of Chicago is located on the Calumet River. It has the capability of handling ocean ships from its location at the western terminus of the St. Lawrence Seaway. Along the waterway, grain elevators transfer farm products to foreign and domestic ships.

Iron and Steel Products Inc. scrapped "anything containing IRON or STEEL." The company often scrapped wooden boxcars. Frequently, Hegewisch residents used salvaged wood from the boxcars to build houses.

Great Lakes Dredge and Dock Company did a great deal of work along the waterways of the Southeast Side. It was necessary to dredge the rivers to maintain their depth. The company often built docks and other waterside improvements. Pile Driver No. 81 is pictured here in 1915.

The *Daily Calumet* staff is pictured here in 1910. The Daily Calumet Publishing Company produced a community newspaper which advertised itself as "the Nation's Oldest Daily Community Newspaper." Established in 1881, the *Daily Southtown* bought it out in the late 1980s, ending the *Daily Calumet's* long run on the Southeast Side.

This is a photograph of the South Chicago Brewing Company in 1895. Small local breweries once operated in many Chicago neighborhoods. Many served specific ethnic groups and local communities by operating or franchising their own saloons. With changes in the industry and economy, most have disappeared over time.

The Steel Workers Organizing Committee (SWOC) attempted to unionize the steel industry in the 1930s. Although U.S. Steel signed a contract with SWOC in 1937, Republic Steel and other smaller companies refused. A strike against these companies began in early May 1937. On Memorial Day 1937, strikers and their families marched toward the entrance of the mill, which housed non-union workers protected by police officers.

Shots rang out as police and strikers confronted each other. Off-duty Chicago police employed by Republic Steel fired approximately 200 shots in about 15 seconds. Ten strikers died, shot in the back or side. One hundred and twenty-five people were injured, including 35 police officers. The Memorial Day Massacre broke the union, but the United Steelworkers gained recognition in the 1940s.

Senator LaFollette's committee investigated the incident and stated, "wounded prisoners of war might have expected and received greater solicitude." A plaque in the parking lot of Memorial Hall, Local 1033, located at 117th and Avenue O, commemorates the Memorial Day Massacre. The plaque lists the names of the ten victims of the incident.

Local 65 of the United Steel Workers of America represented workers at the South Works. The local involved itself in the local community by participating in parades and other activities. Local 65 built a union hall at 94th and South Chicago Avenue, which was used for union meetings and rented out for private affairs.

Local 1033 of the United Steel Workers of America represented the workers at Republic Steel. These employees picketed during a 1946 strike. Memories of recent events like the Depression and the war are obvious in the wording of the signs.

When they occurred, strikes had a major impact on the surrounding community. One of the most serious strikes took place in 1959. Here, picketers parade in front of the U.S. Steel South Works plant.

Union elections were often as hotly contested as political elections. Ed Sadlowski joined the United Steel Workers of America in 1956 as an employee at the South Works. In 1964, he upset the incumbent and won the election to become president of Local 65. In January 1975, he became District 31 director, the largest district in the USWA. This photo shows Ed Sadlowski campaigning at the Interlake Steel Plant on the East Side.

Ed Sadlowski ran for the national presidency of the USWA in February 1977 as a reform candidate against Lloyd McBride, who had been endorsed by retiring Union President I.W. Abel. Although Sadlowski received high vote totals in the Chicago District, he lost the election. In this photo, local union members show their support for the Sadlowski candidacy.

Four

CHURCHES

While smokestacks, grain elevators, and the Chicago Skyway form much of Southeast Chicago's skyline, they do not go unchallenged for dominance. The churches of the steel district raise splendid spires in competition with the colossal structures of the district's industrial might. Churches played a crucial role in the development of a sense of community in Southeast Chicago. They provided a home for the various ethnic communities that came to the Steel District by not only furnishing places of worship, but also community centers. Here, immigrants, their children, and grandchildren could pray in the age old tradition of the homeland. Church bells called steelworkers to a higher reality and an ancient ritual. In church and in the church hall, residents could celebrate with members of their ethnic group. They could plan futures and pray to God in their own ways. Beautiful church interiors provided an escape from the gray mills and crowded wooden two-flats of the Bush, Irondale, and Slag Valley. The parish would later give these same communities a solid base for improving their position in that industrial world.

St. Michael Archangel Catholic Church celebrated its Golden Jubilee in 1942 with a solemn high Mass offered by Father John Lange. The ancient Latin ritual of the Mass provided a common experience for Roman Catholics from all ethnic groups. Reverend Lange served as pastor of St. Michael's for 45 years until his death on September 26, 1960. The Vatican named him Monsignor in March 1946.

Roman Catholics founded the Southeast Side's first church, St. Patrick's, in 1857 as a territorial parish for English speaking Catholics, mostly Irish. Originally located at 93rd and Houston Avenue in South Chicago, the parish moved to 95th and Commercial Avenue in 1877. After a fire in 1903, parishioners built the structure in this photo. Pictured from left to right are the church, school, and rectory as seen in 1934.

South Chicago German residents formed Immanuel Lutheran Church in 1873. Originally named the First Evangelical Lutheran Church of South Chicago, it stood at 9031 South Houston Avenue. The architectural firm, Worthman and Steinbach, designed the Gothic Revival church completed in 1907.

Lutherans organized the first church on the East Side, Bethlehem Lutheran Church, in 1874. The district was then known as Colehour, after a local real estate developer. The parish later rented out the old church building, seen here in an 1876 photo, as the first home of Gallistel School.

On Holy Thursday, 1918, disaster struck Bethlehem Lutheran. A crowd watched in horror as the church burned down. A few days later, on Easter, the congregation resolved to build a new church and school, presently located at 103rd and Avenue H.

The First Church Evangelical Association, a group of German and Swedish Methodists, organized a congregation in 1875 as the East Side's second church. Their first home, pictured here, stood near 99th and Avenue J. Later, a second church was established at 103rd and Ewing Avenue. Currently named the East Side United Methodist Church, it is now located at 11000 Ewing Avenue.

Swedish Lutherans established Bethany Lutheran Church in South Chicago in 1881. Parishioners built a wooden structure first, and added a brick veneer in 1900. Erick Gustaf Petterson designed the Gothic Revival church at 9118 South Houston. This interior view of the church was taken in 1925.

Polish Catholic steelworkers established the first Polish congregation on the Southeast Side, Immaculate Conception, in 1882 as an ethnic parish. Eventually, four Polish Catholic parishes served the large Polish community of South Chicago. Pictured here is the ornate Marian altar of the church located at 88th and Commercial Avenue.

German Catholics organized Saints Peter and Paul Church in 1882. Parishioners celebrated the first Mass in a vacant store at 92nd and Commercial Avenue. The German Catholic community built a new church and rectory, shown here in a postcard with a 1910 postmark, at 91st and Exchange Avenue.

Catholics founded Saint Kevin's Church as an outgrowth of St. Patrick's Church to serve the growing Catholic population of South Deering. The original church building was built in 1884. The St. Stephen Social Club is pictured here in front of the church in the 1920s. The parish dedicated a new combination church, school, and parish hall building on September 19, 1926.

St. Columba Church, 133 and Green Bay Avenue, Hegewisch, Ill.

Hegewisch Catholics formed St. Columba Church as a territorial Catholic parish in 1884. They built a frame structure, shown here at 13305 Greenbay Avenue, in 1886. The building was later raised, and a residence was built under the church. The resulting staircase proved to be a pallbearer's nightmare. The inset shows Father Chodniewicz, pastor of St. Columba, in 1904. Shortly thereafter, Fr. Chodniewicz established a Polish parish in Hegewisch named after his patron saint, St. Florian.

Methodists established the Hegewisch Methodist Church in 1885. They originally held services over a store before building a small church at 13315 South Brandon Avenue. In 1905, the congregation sold the structure and temporarily held services in the second story of the Hegewisch Opera House. In 1906, the assembly dedicated the new church, which is pictured here.

St. Francis De Sales Catholic Church primarily cared for the German and Luxemburger communities. This frame church served the congregation from its founding in 1889 until 1910, when the parish constructed a new combination church and school building. On January 23, 1925, a fire almost totally destroyed the new church. This supposedly destroyed the health of the pastor, Rev. John Suerth, who had just paid off the indebtedness of the church.

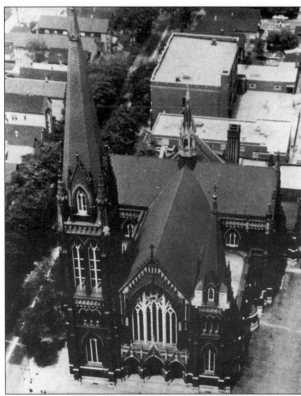

In 1892, Polish Catholics founded St. Michael Archangel Parish at 83rd and South Shore Drive to serve the Polish families of South Chicago's "Bush." This aerial view shows the cruciform Gothic Revival structure with its 250-foot steeple designed by architect William Brinkman in 1907. F.X. Zettler of Munich, Germany, designed the large Gothic arched stained-glass windows.

This midnight Mass was held at St. Michael's on Christmas Eve, 1982. St. Michael's conducts services in Polish, Spanish, and English to accommodate the changing ethnic makeup of the parish.

The Agudath Achim-Bikur Cholim Synagogue originally served East European Jewish shopkeepers and steelworkers in the South Chicago community. The Litvaker community organized the synagogue, located at 8927 South Houston Avenue, in 1902. Now the home of a Black-Jewish congregation, it is the oldest continuously operating synagogue in the city. Architect Henry Newhouse designed the Romanesque structure.

This building is St. Florian's Catholic Church, located at 132nd and Houston Avenue. The next building is a combination church and school building constructed in 1927. A third building in the photo belongs to a Protestant congregation. Father Florian Chodniewicz organized St. Florian in 1905 to serve Hegewisch's Poles.

Croatians formed Sacred Heart Parish in 1913 for Croatian Catholics who originally worshipped at St. George's Slovenian Catholic Church on the East Side. It was the third Croatian parish in Chicago. The photo shows the dedication of the original church on May 17, 1914.

Serbian immigrants founded St. Michael Archangel Serbian Orthodox Church in 1919. Shown in this photo from 1982 is the interior of the church at 98th and Commercial Avenue designed by Franz Roy in 1926. Seventy-nine years of Orthodox Serbian worship on Commercial Avenue came to an end on July 2, 1998, when the congregation moved to the Serbian Social Center it built in 1986 in south suburban Lansing. Worshippers hope to build a new church adjacent to the social center.

Mexicans from across the Southeast Side gathered for the dedication of Our Lady of Guadalupe Church in 1928. In about 1923, Rev. William Kane, S.J. began to minister to South Chicago's Mexicans. In 1924, the Claretian Fathers came to the district to staff this church which was the oldest Mexican parish in Chicago. The church provides the site for the National Shrine of St. Jude, the solemn novenas to St. Jude, and the St. Jude League for Catholic policemen.

This photo shows Our Lady of Guadalupe Church, which opened in 1928. Its Classical Revival building was designed by architect James Burns. The parish began operation of a kindergarten program staffed by the Cordi-Marian Sisters from Mexico in 1928. In 1948, the Sisters of St. Francis from Joliet opened a parochial school while the Cordi-Marian Sisters continued social and catechetical work.

Ten members of the New Hope Missionary Baptist Church founded Pilgrim Baptist Church in 1917. It is one of the oldest African-American churches on the Southeast Side. This photo shows Zion Evangelical Lutheran Church which closed, and the Pilgrim Baptist congregation purchased the building in September 1946. Pilgrim Baptist provided the location of a famous gospel music scene from the original *Blues Brothers* movie, which was partially filmed on the Southeast Side of Chicago.

Post-World War II Serbian immigrants organized St. Simeon Mirotocivi Serbian Orthodox Church in 1964. They left St. Michael the Archangel Church during a brief schism in the Serbian Orthodox Church, which ended in 1992. The building is a reproduction of the 15th-century Serbian monastery of Kalenich. The architects area Pavlecic, Kovacevic and Markovich and the style is the Morava School of Serbian Byzantine Architecture. This is a sketch of the building drawn by local artist Joseph Mulac.

Five

SCHOOLS

Bowm School Class 1880. miss Jennie L Teacher

Schools, both public and parochial, have played a crucial role in the development of community in Southeast Chicago. Many of these schools started out as small ventures operating at a low budget. The first public school in the Irondale neighborhood of South Deering opened in a rented building on Torrence Avenue in 1876 just after the opening of the Brown Steel and Iron Works. Later that year, a two-room school opened on 107th and Hoxie. In 1884, the Cummings Public School began operation on 107th and Bensley. The Bright School replaced it in 1922. In South Chicago, the Bowen School served as both an elementary and high school, eventually developing into a large public high school educating Southeast Side youth. Washington High School opened in the late 1950s to serve the East Side and Hegewisch. Parochial schools arrived with the first Roman Catholic parish, St. Patrick's, in 1857. Eventually, a series of Catholic parochial school opened serving the various different ethnic communities. At its height, the Polish Catholic community operated five parochial schools and a Polish Catholic high school, St. Michael's in Southeast Chicago.

The first school in the area was the South Chicago School, founded in 1862 by Charles I. Parker. Bowen School, located at 93rd and Houston, replaced it in 1876 and served students of both elementary and high school grades. The 1880 class pictured here poses with teacher Miss Jennie Logan in front of the entrance to the school.

Residents named the first Bowen School, shown here, for James H. Bowen, the "Father of South Chicago." Mr. Bowen founded the Calumet and Chicago Canal and Dock Company to develop the harbor facilities of the Calumet River. The improvement of the Calumet River paved the way for industries to locate in the area.

A new high school, Bowen High School, opened in 1910. Located at 2710 East 89th Street, the school was an imitation of Schurz High School, a North Side landmark building designed by Dwight Perkins, a Prairie School contemporary of Frank Lloyd Wright. The five-story, 1,400-student building, complete with metal shops, laboratories, and an 818 seat auditorium, cost roughly $600,000 to construct.

Bowen offered a full schedule of curricular and extra-curricular activities. The cheerleading squad of 1942 supported the athletic teams of the school. Pictured in the top row are as follows: Anna Bugos, P. Fattore, M. Dusek, T. Martin, B. Conners, I. Gronkiewicz, M. Bednarski. The bottom row includes M. Martin, M. Leverich, and G. Shiparski.

The 1917 Bowen football team lines up in a "T" formation. According to the school yearbook, *The Bowen Prep*, the 1917 season was a very successful one. Bowen's lightweight division football team lost 15-14 in the city championship game against North Side rival Senn High School.

Ethnic groups organized clubs such as the Latones Club of Bowen High School, shown here in 1948, to help perpetuate ethnic solidarity and pride. There has always been concern that the children of immigrants would lose the culture and traditions of their parents.

Bowen High School students took part in many extra-curricular activities. These Drama Club members pose in costumes for an upcoming production in the 1940s.

Originally opened in 1888, the Phil Sheridan Elementary School, a "feeder" school for Bowen High School, is located on the 9000 block of Exchange Avenue. The variety of architectural styles in the school building, shown here in 1940, reflect the numerous additions added at various times to accommodate the growing population of South Chicago.

The Sullivan Elementary School opened in 1892. The 1902 school building pictured in this view stands on 83rd Street near South Shore Boulevard, across the street from the swimming pool and field house of Russell Square Park.

In 1870, South Chicagoans built a four-room wooden schoolhouse at 89th and Superior Avenue. The Chicago Board of Education later rebuilt the school and named it the J.N. Thorp Elementary School. This photo shows the multi-ethnic male graduation class from June 1933.

Pictured here are the female graduates of the Thorp School in 1933. The Thorp School stood near to the early African-American area of South Chicago. African Americans lived in an area of South Chicago near the 89th Street entrance to South Works called "Millgate." The first African Americans moved into the area around the turn of the century.

The Bright School, dedicated in January 1924, serves the South Deering neighborhood. Originally named the Cummings School, it held classes in a two-room building located at 107th and Hoxie in 1884. After the Calumet Iron and Steel Company, owned by J.C. Cummings, purchased the Joseph H. Brown steel mill, postal authorities changed the name of the local post office to Cummings. Pictured here are students in the 1930s.

The Marsh School was located at 98th and Exchange in the South Deering neighborhood. Built in 1910, it originally served the community that spread south along Commercial Avenue from South Chicago. Its enrollment increased when the post World War II housing boom led to the building of numerous home in the Veterans Memorial Park area west of the school.

Residents named the Douglas Taylor School, located at 99th and Avenue H on the East Side, for an early real estate developer. The school stood in an area known as "Taylorville," which, at that time, was part of the Village of Hyde Park. Pictured here is the 1913 Taylor Graduation Class.

The Gallistel School, located at 103rd and Ewing Avenue, opened as the first school on the East Side on land donated by Mathew W. Gallistel, a local businessman who came to Chicago from Austria in 1855. Gallistel moved to the Colehour neighborhood in the East Side in 1873. He served as postmaster and president of the South Chicago Board of Education.

The Daniel Webster School served the Hegewisch neighborhood. The original building, constructed on swamp land in 1886, had only eight rooms. The board of education tore it down in June 1917 and replaced it with the Henry Clay School. Residents described the Webster School, pictured here, as a "veritable fire trap."

In 1906, the Webster School (later Clay School) faculty included the following, from left to right: (front row) unidentified; Miss Krietwitz, teacher; Miss Lamb, teacher; and Mr. Monahan, principal; (back row) Mr. Martindale, custodian; Miss Maxey, teacher; unidentified; unidentified; and Miss Jabrosky, teacher. Mr. Martindale wore a star and served as combination custodian, truant officer, and all around "right-hand man." Most of the teachers arrived in Hegewisch by train each day. When trains were late, Mr. Martindale started classes.

St. Patrick's not only established an elementary school to serve its predominantly Irish population, but also opened a high school in 1889. It was the first Catholic coeducational parish high school in the city of Chicago. In 1924, the high school consolidated with Mercy High School. This is the 1949 graduation class of St. Patrick's Grammar School.

Virtually every Catholic parish on the Southeast Side had an elementary school. Many Catholics felt that Protestants dominated the public schools, so Catholic schools also served the particular ethnic group who attended that parish. The 1910 class of SS. Peter and Paul parish pose for a class photo. The school opened on November 25, 1882, and served the predominantly German Catholic community of South Chicago.

The Sacred Heart School class of 1930 is pictured here with the pastor, Rev. Bono Andacic, OFM. The church and school served Croatian Catholics in the Southeast Side community. It is located at 96th and Escanaba Avenue in the South Deering neighborhood.

Father Matthew Fisher, pastor, and students from the eighth-grade class of St. Francis De Sales School pose in front of the school in this 1946 photo. St. Francis recently closed its elementary school, reflecting a common occurrence in many changing Chicago neighborhoods. St. Francis De Sales High School has remained open and is the only Catholic high school left on the Southeast Side. St. Patrick's, SS. Peter and Paul, and St. Michael's Catholic high schools have all closed.

Religious ceremonies marked important turning points in the lives of Catholic school students. This is the St. George Confirmation Class of 1919. St. George's parish on the East Side served the Slovenian community. Italians and Croatians also worshipped at St. George's until Sacred Heart parish opened in 1913.

St. Florian School served the Polish Catholic community in Hegewisch. The 1932 graduating class gives one an idea of the size of some of the Catholic parishes in the community. The priest pictured with the graduates is the Father Vincent Nowicki who served as pastor from 1922 until 1933.

Six

SOCIAL LIFE

The various neighborhoods and ethnic communities of Southeast Chicago maintained a varied social life that included ethnic gatherings, neighborhood parades, and local celebrations of national holidays. Southeast Chicago residents supported a host of social organizations including lodges, ethnic fraternal groups, women's clubs, neighborhood improvement organizations, boys clubs, veteran's organizations, scout troops, and sports teams, as well as other manifestations of community. Some of these celebrated ethnicity, parish life, or organized labor. Others allowed inhabitants to celebrate their common connection to Southeast Chicago neighborhoods. These helped to create both an active social life and a sense of identity, pride, and loyalty based on residency. All helped to create a sense of unity both within and beyond ethnic boundaries. Most also provided a good time for residents.

Parades and community celebrations were important events in the social life of the various Southeast Side neighborhoods. Public presentations of neighborhood pride were common.

The photograph shows a 1955 Memorial Day parade on the 13300 block of Baltimore Avenue. The group leading the parade is the Hegewisch Raiders Drum and Bugle Corps.

Members of the group "Del Coro" participate in the Mexican Independence Day parade in South Chicago on September 15, 1957. They are dressed in Mariachi apparel to reflect their Mexican heritage. The South Chicago Mexican community is one of the oldest in the city of Chicago. South Chicago's Mexican Independence Day celebration continues to be a much-anticipated local event.

Under the leadership of Joe Grande, the Fourth of July celebration sponsored by the South Deering Improvement Association provided the social event of the year for the neighborhood. This photo shows a float is being prepared for the parade in 1938. In addition to the parade, the celebration included a beauty contest and a spectacular fireworks show at Trumbull Park.

Members of the South Deering Improvement Association sponsored numerous softball tournaments. This photo shows members of the Trumbull Park Labor Day Softball Tournament Committee behind the trophy table on Labor Day, 1962. Pictured from left to right are Mario DiCicco, Joseph Kral, Emil De Giacomo, Joseph Gornick, Louis Dinocenzo, Tony Lowery, John Ciganovich, Joseph Grande, Theo Zawlinski, John Brass, and Andrew Diorio.

The East Side celebrated "Old Fashioned Days" with a summer sidewalk sale and other activities, including the election of the "Mayor of the East Side." This view from the early 1960s shows participants of the event, including 10th Ward Alderman Emil Pacini (third from the left), "Mayor of the East Side" and current 10th Ward Alderman John Buchanan (fourth from the left), and Richard J. Daley Mayor of Chicago (center).

The Labor Day celebration at Calumet Park on the East Side provided fun and a sense of community for residents. Activities included a parade, picnic, drum and bugle corps competition, concert, and beauty contest. Pictured here are contestants from a Miss East Side Beauty contest held for the 1965 Labor Day Celebration.

Many of the community celebrations honored veterans and patriotic events. This photo shows a 1926 Flag Day Parade in Hegewisch. Participants marched down the 132nd block of Baltimore Avenue.

Numerous community clubs and organizations contributed to an active local social life. The East Side Maroon, a social and athletic club, sponsored many activities including the popular "truck party." Since many members of the club did not own their own automobiles, trucks used commercially during the week were pressed into service to provide transportation.

The Cherokee Athletic Club was another East Side institution. Athletic clubs, which were very popular in Chicago, were often referred to as social and athletic clubs or SACs. They grew out of children's play groups or from gangs. In many parts of the city they played important roles in local political organizations.

Neighborhood parks helped to organize local clubs. The Old Timers Club from Russell Square Park poses for a photo in the park across the street from Sullivan School. Local 65 of the Steelworkers Union sponsored this mushroom hunt party on October 2, 1952. Unions played important social roles in the community.

Girls enjoy the merry-go-round at St. Columba's Parish Carnival c. 1950. Parish carnivals helped raise funds for local churches and produced important social events for the community.

The Knight of Pythias enjoy a day at their 1918 picnic. The membership of the Knights of Pythias, E.C. Race Lodge, was mainly comprised of German and Swedish Protestants. The lodge involved itself in social activities and community service work. Notice the organization's hats held by members.

Children also had an opportunity to join community organizations. Pictured here is the East Side First Evangelical Church Girl Scout Troop 102, one of the oldest troops in the community. Local churches sponsored most scout troops.

Masons dedicated the South Chicago Masonic Lodge, located at 91st and Exchange Avenue, in the winter of 1918. As the neighborhood changed, the membership of the Masons declined and the lodge eventually sold the building to another important community organization, the Mexican Community Committee (MCC). The MCC, founded in 1959, originally developed as a delinquency prevention group. Currently, the MCC sponsors numerous educational, social, and cultural activities for the Mexican community.

German Baptists organized the South Chicago YMCA on May 15, 1882. After being located at several sites in the community and then closing for awhile due to financial difficulties, a permanent South Chicago facility opened on November 6, 1926. The "Y" offered rooms, Americanization classes, and both social and athletic activities. Here, volleyball players enjoy a game in the YMCA gymnasium.

Parks offered numerous opportunities for community residents. In 1926, these girls participated in a Calumet Park recreational program, performing an activity called "pyramids."

Lake Michigan provided additional recreational opportunities for local residents. Ora Matthews Coon and her brothers Warren and Wayne spent a day at the beach at Calumet Park in June 1917. Notice the styles of the swimsuits worn by the visitors to the beach.

In addition to major parks, smaller playgrounds and playlots were scattered throughout the community. On Flag Day, children participated in activities at the Rowan Playground on the East Side.

The South Chicago Neighborhood House has been helping the people of the "Bush" since 1911. The American Baptist Church originally opened the settlement house, later affiliated with the Hull House organization founded by Jane Addams. The agency provides numerous social services to neighborhood residents including counseling programs. This photo shows a 1982 street fair to raise funds for the house near the South Works mill.

Athletic activities and teams, such as this YMCA basketball team from 1897, were important to the social life of the community. In its earlier years, Roman Catholics viewed the YMCA as a Protestant organization that might attempt to convert Catholic youth. For this reason, many Catholic priests discouraged and even forbade parishioners from participating in activities at the South Chicago YMCA.

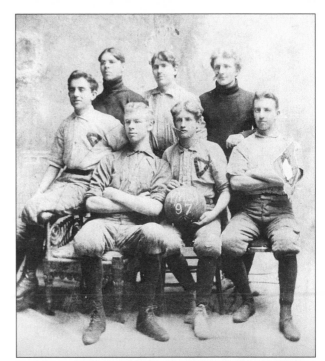

Churches and ethnic organizations sponsored many sports teams. This is a team picture of the Calumet District Sunday School Athletic Association heavyweight basketball champions in 1914–15, who were sponsored by the East Side Swedish Mission. Churches often used athletic teams to encourage regular church attendance and participation by younger members of the congregation.

The East Side Boosters baseball team played their home games at Calumet Park. This 1932 photo includes James Fitzgibbons (top row, far right), the founder of the East Side Historical Society (now the Southeast Historical Society). Fitzgibbons coached several youth baseball teams during his lifetime of community service.

The St. Florian KSKJ baseball team hailed from St. George's parish. This Slovenian organization sponsored many activities for its members. Pictured here is the 1933 national championship baseball team.

Felix Buoscio, a young Italian who later became a judge, founded The Bonivirs SAC (Social and Athletic Club) in 1917 to provide activities for young Italians in the area. The Bonivirs ("good man") sponsored athletic teams, dances, and other activities. Pictured here is the 1961 Bonivir football team. The Bonivirs received a state charter in 1924, and remained in existence until the mid-1970s.

On the Southeast Side, bowling developed as a popular local sport. Many bowling alleys in the various neighborhoods supported the different leagues and teams. The South Chicago Bowling Club was one of the oldest bowling organizations in Illinois.

The Southeast Sportsmen's Club met in Hegewisch on the shores of Wolf Lake. Members formed the club in 1938 for the "conservation and propagation of our wildlife and natural resources." Among the sporting and recreational activities conducted by the club were hunting, fishing, and trapshooting. The fox hunt pictured here took place in 1948.

Even in the shadows of the area factories, fishing along the shore of Lake Michigan was a favorite method of relaxation for local residents. Pictured here in the early 1980s, is a fisherman with the Commonwealth Edison State Line Generating Plant visible in the background.

Boxing was always a favorite neighborhood spectator sport. In this photo from 1912, Jack O'Keefe (left) and Tim O'Neill (right) square off at the South Deering Pleasure and Athletic Club at 10558 South Torrence.

On occasion, a neighborhood boxer moved on to a high profile professional career. "Battling Nelson," also known as the "Durable Dane," came from Hegewisch. Nelson appears here preparing for a fight against Joe Gans in Nevada in 1906. Nelson lost the fight on a foul in the 42nd round. Two years later, he won the world lightweight title by knocking out Gans twice in two months.

The Calumet River, usually thought of as a "working river" due to the large number of commercial and industrial facilities located on it, also furnished a site for recreational activities. The Harbor Lights Boat Club was one of many yacht clubs located on the Calumet River.

The Roby Race track operated at 108th Street and the state line. Pictured here is the starting line at a 1918 race. Al Karp, driving Number 14, won the race. A fatal accident in August 1936, followed by a second accident on September 20, 1936, when a car ran into the stands, resulted in the track's closing.

Seven

FAMILIES IN GOOD TIMES AND BAD

Families have played a central role in the history of Southeast Chicago. They created neighborhoods, preserved traditions while developing new ones, and established social institutions. Along with family, ethnicity played a crucial role in the development of the Steel District's identity. Southeast Chicago was, and continues to be, the recipient of wave after wave of immigrant arrivals. Early white settlers found the area inhabited by the Potawatomi Nation.

These native-born whites soon found themselves joined by immigrants from Ireland, Britain, Germany, and Sweden. Then came waves of Eastern and Southern Europeans, including Poles, Slovenians, Serbs, Croatians, and Italians. Shortly afterwards came African Americans and Mexicans. Over time, each of these racial and ethnic groups left their marks on the family, religious, social, and political traditions of Southeast Chicago.

Finally, both Southeast Chicago and its families have been touched by war. Along with the family celebrations pictured in this chapter are liberty bond rallies, victory gardens, war workers, veterans groups, and those who died for their country.

Four generations of women from the family of John Walsh, the first principal of Bowen School, appear in this photograph from 1890. The women are Mrs. McGovern (great grandmother), Mrs. Margaret Walsh (grandmother), Mrs. Margaret Kidden (daughter), and Frances Kidden (granddaughter).

These women comprise three generations from one of Hegewisch's earliest families. The family originally lived along Wolf Lake for 63 years, renting out boats for use on the lake to fishermen. Minnie Lighfoot is pictured standing, Annie Neubeiser is seated in the dark dress, and Fredrika Konybisy is seated with a shawl over her shoulders. Mrs. Konybisy received a letter from Franklin D. Roosevelt on the occasion of her 100th birthday on January 20, 1938.

The Bacilio Hernandez and Paula Hernandez-Valencia family was one of the first families of Mexican descent to live in South Deering. This portrait was taken about 1942. The children pictured are (not in order) Harold, Rose, Augustine, Amelia, Leonard, Mary, and Thomas.

Millie, Ray, Connie, and Henry Dolatowski were children of Polish immigrants. Family ties were very important to many of the ethnic groups on the Southeast Side and often included the extended family. Many times, one family member would come to the States and begin saving passage money for other members, afterwards sending for them until the entire family lived in America.

Twenty-year-old Olga Smith Osterberg and five-year-old Mabel Smith pose for a photographer. The Osterbergs were one of the earliest Swedish families to come to the East Side. Immigration patterns on the Southeast Side reflected those of the rest of the country. Earliest immigrants included Irish, German, and Swedish families.

113

The Maloney family, of Irish descent, poses for a family portrait. The Irish, German, and Swedish immigrants were followed by Poles, Italians, Lithuanians, Slovenians, Serbians, Croatians, Greeks, and others. In turn, they were followed by Mexicans and African Americans migrating to the urban, industrial North from the rural, agricultural South.

This photograph of a family picnic at 110th Street in 1900 shows the rural nature of much of the East Side at the time. Later, single family homes covered the area.

The *charivari,* or in Polish, *Kocia Muzyka,* was a well-established European tradition. Merrymakers blew horns, beat drums, and followed the wedding party down the streets, often presenting the bride with a baby carriage. The *Kocia Muzyka* pictured honored the wedding of Josephine Nowak and Edmund Czosnowski at Immaculate Conception Church, whose spire appears in the background.

This photograph of the Spretnjac wedding in 1920 signifies the importance of family events. A wedding was an opportunity to escape the drudgery of daily existence to celebrate. Depending on one's cultural or ethnic background, some wedding celebrations might last for days.

Mourners attend a funeral at St. Joseph's Catholic Church, located at 8801 South Saginaw Avenue, a parish founded in 1900 by Lithuanians. The final rite of passage played an important role in ethnic communities. Wakes often lasted several days, and families remembered the dead in memorial services for years. Various ethnic groups founded their own cemeteries.

First Holy Communion celebrations provided an important rite of passage for many religions, especially Catholics. This is a photograph of the 1882 First Communion class of SS. Peter and Paul Catholic Church of South Chicago. A parish priest and a sister from the Third Order of St. Francis of Mary Immaculate are present. Nuns made contributions that gave Catholic parishes the ability to afford the cost of providing educational services to parish families.

The Polish, Chor Wolnosc (Choir of Freedom), pictured *c.* 1920, sang throughout the Southeast Side until the 1940s. Ethnic choirs celebrated traditional ethnic music. Like theater groups, dance groups, and poetry circles, they helped to preserve cultural traditions. Many of these groups no longer exist due to dwindling membership among the younger members of the ethnic communities.

Ethnic groups formed various fraternal, cultural, and patriotic organizations on the Southeast Side. Many of these groups patterned themselves on the German Turnverein societies. The Hrvatski Sokol (Croatian Falcons) met in Croatian Hall at 96th and Commercial Avenue. Sokol members believed in physical fitness and patriotism.

The Slovenian Band from St. George's Church marches in a parade. Ethnic bands allowed members to perform for the community at large and maintained a sense of ethnic identity and pride.

The church was the center of family and social life for most ethnic groups. Joseph and Joanne Vukobratovich were married in a ceremony at St. Michael the Archangel Serbian Orthodox Church in the early 1980s.

Immigrants from Luxembourg came to the Southeast Side. Often, outsiders include Luxembourgers with German Catholics. Many area Luxembourgers attended St. Francis De Sales Parish and formed their own ethnic organizations such as the Luxembourg Brotherhood, pictured here in a 1930 photograph.

Italian Americans formed the Roman Knights social and civic club in South Deering. Artist Joseph Mulac's sketch shows their original meeting place at 10625 Hoxie. The group officially received its charter from the State of Illinois on March 1, 1932. Founders hoped to keep young men off street corners and out of trouble during the Depression. Andrew Diorio served as the Knights first president. The current president is Alex Savastano.

In 1933, Rev. John Lange, pastor of St. Michael's Polish Roman Catholic Church, and University of Chicago sociologist Clifford Shaw organized the St. Michael's Boys Club in the Bush neighborhood. As part of the pioneering Chicago Area Project, the boys club formed the nucleus for the Russell Square Community Committee, an organization led by Steve Bubacz that combated juvenile delinquency in South Chicago.

Many of the ethnic groups continued to have strong ties with relatives and friends in their native country by maintaining many traditions. In this photo from the 1940s, Martha Martinez models a Mexican dress on her back porch in South Deering.

Mexican equestrians ride in a parade on 91st and Commercial Avenue in 1982. Ethnic celebrations like Mexican Independence Day and Cinco de Mayo were popular events not only with the Mexican community but also with other ethnic groups in the community.

Neighborhood children work on a mural sponsored by the SCOPE (South Chicago Organized People's Effort), located at 9000 S. Buffalo in the early 1980s. African-American residents organized SCOPE in 1970 to provide activities for local youth. An African-American community appeared early in South Chicago near the South Works at 90th and Green Bay Avenue.

The Southeast Side played an important role in U.S. efforts during numerous wars both in terms of military service as well as the home front. In this photograph, workers from Pressed Steel in Hegewisch attend a Liberty Bond Rally in 1918.

Members of the Hegewisch Red Cross Auxiliary and other residents conducted a bond rally at 133rd and Baltimore Avenue during the First World War. Bond rallies raised much-needed funds to help support the war effort.

The steel mills and factories on the Southeast Side produced the materials crucial to the success of the military in battle. In this photograph, shell casings are stacked up in the yard at Western Steel in Hegewisch in 1918.

Area residents contributed to the war effort in many ways. Victory gardens provided a method by which ordinary people could help the cause. Proud residents pose at the South Chicago Victory Gardens located in the Cheltenham area just north of the community.

When soldiers returned to civilian life they often joined veterans organizations. There were numerous such organizations on the Southeast Side. The American Legion, Veterans of Foreign Wars, Polish Legion of American Veterans, and others met in all of the neighborhoods of the area. Members of the American Legion Illiana Post 220 burned the mortgage to their meeting hall on October 11, 1940.

Kitty Kalwasinski Markovich and Florence Josephs worked at U.S. Steel South Works in 1945. Many women entered the steel mills during WW II to help the war effort. The names on the welder's helmet are those of her brothers serving in the armed forces. The solid star signifies that her brother Frank died in action in France.

This Civil Defense parade on the 8800 block of Commercial in 1943 drew many spectators. Local parades and celebrations boosted civilian morale during WW II.

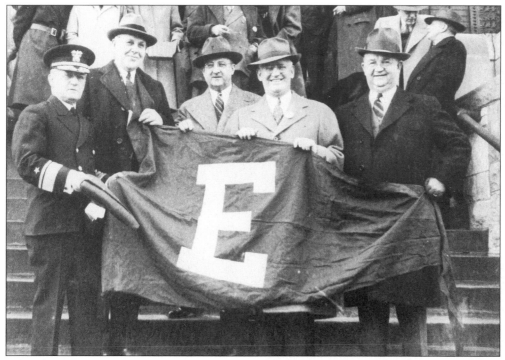

Officials of the United States Navy present the "E" pennant to South Works management on March 19, 1942. Steel production was critical to defense during WW II. The federal government awarded this pennant to South Works as a recognition of efficient steel production at the mill.

Workers at the Pressed Steel plant in Hegewisch during WW II manufactured this "Big Shot" mechanized howitzer. Pressed Steel normally built railroad cars, but turned to producing armaments during the war.

Residents established a veteran's memorial at Wolf Lake State Park in September, 1946. The memorial consisted of trees planted near stone markers sponsored by over 100 area veteran's organizations. In this photograph, a contingent from the Hegewisch Polish Legion of American Veterans marches in the dedication parade. Recently, students from Washington High School uncovered and restored the markers.

Carmel B. Harvey lived in Hegewisch and graduated from Washington High School in 1965. He died in combat in Vietnam while saving two wounded comrades. Harvey received the Congressional Medal of Honor for his heroic actions.

Southeast Siders have always served their country. The parish of Our Lady of Guadalupe in South Chicago suffered more war dead during the Vietnam War than any other Catholic parish in the United States. This monument erected in 1970 stands in memory of the supreme sacrifice of 12 parishioners. It is located across the street from the church at 91st Street and Brandon in South Chicago.

ACKNOWLEDGMENTS

This book is dedicated to Mirron "Mike" Alexandroff, President Emeritus of Columbia College/Chicago, and to the memory of James P. Fitzgibbons of the East Side.

A discussion in the late 1970s between Mike Alexandroff, Paul Johnson of Columbia College, and Ed Sadlowski of the United Steelworkers led to the Southeast Chicago Historical Project, which for much of the early 1980s helped Southeast Side residents collect and tell their own history. Led by James R. Martin, Project Director, and Associate Director Dominic A. Pacyga, the project was funded by Columbia College, the National Endowment for the Humanities, and the Illinois Humanities Council, and aided in the creation of a large archive which included a wonderful collection of historic and contemporary photographs. This corpus is now deposited with the James P. Fitzgibbons Museum in Calumet Park on Chicago's Southeast Side, where it continues to grow and help residents tell the story of Chicago's Steel District.

Many institutions, businesses, individuals, and families helped with the Southeast Chicago Historical Project and thus with this book. We would like to thank Bert Gall, Lya Dym Rosenblum, and Shelley Brown of Columbia College. Jim Sulski, Yvonne Gonzalez, James Klekowski, and Tony Perez all worked both as Columbia College students and as staff on the project. Ed Sadlowski was not only an inspiration for the project, but offered help and encouragement in detailing the role that organized labor played in these communities. The late great Jim Fitzgibbons helped in more ways than could ever be told. The gone, but not forgotten *Daily Calumet* and its editor Bob Bong offered assistance and let us run a weekly historical column. United States Steel Corporation (now USX) volunteered historical photos and records. Hundreds of residents made this book possible by opening up their personal photo albums and family histories. We cannot mention them all, but wish to thank in particular Walter Maloney, Auggie Ruf Sr., the Buoscio family, the Dolatowski family, the Lange family, Carmen J. Arias, Maria Ofelia Torres, Henry Martinez, and Joseph Mulac.

In addition, we would like to thank the following for their assistance in preparing this book on Chicago's Southeast Side: the staff of the Southeast Historical Society and the James Fitzgibbons Historical Museum, especially Ora Coon, Alex Savastano, and Frank Stanley, and the Museology Class from the Southeast Historical Society, including Lucia Aleman, Liliana Aranda, Aracely Galvan, Miguel Garcia, Chris Guerrero, Vanessa Huizar, Roger Lopez, Brenda Mares, Eduardo Ornelas, Araceli Pantoja, Oswaldo Pimental, Sandra Ramirez, Marissa Segura, and Ronald Walker. We also want to thank Mike and Helen Aniol for sharing their expertise on the Hegewisch neighborhood.

A portion of the royalties from this book will benefit the Southeast Historical Society and the James P. Fitzgibbons Historical Museum.